MAR 16

W9-CKH-168

Rookie Biographies®

Jane Goodall

Champion for Chimpanzees

by Jodie Shepherd

Content Consultant

Nanci R. Vargus, Ed.D.
Professor Emeritus, University of Indianapolis

Reading Consultant

Jeanne M. Clidas, Ph.D.
Reading Specialist

Children's Press®
An Imprint of Scholastic Inc.

Library of Congress Cataloging-in-Publication Data
Shepherd, Jodie.
  Jane Goodall / by Jodie Shepherd.
    pages cm. -- (Rookie biographies)
  Includes index.
  ISBN 978-0-531-21413-8 (library binding) -- ISBN 978-0-531-21426-8 (pbk.) 1. Goodall, Jane,
1934---Juvenile literature. 2. Women primatologists--England--Biography--Juvenile literature. 3.
Chimpanzees--Tanzania--Gombe National Park--Juvenile literature. 4. Wildlife conservation--Juvenile
literature. I. Title.
  QL31.G58S47 2015
  591.092--dc23
  [B]   2015017318

Produced by Spooky Cheetah Press
Design by Keith Plechaty

© 2016 by Scholastic Inc.

Printed in China 62

SCHOLASTIC, CHILDREN'S PRESS, ROOKIE BIOGRAPHIES®, and associated logos are trademarks and/or
registered trademarks of Scholastic Inc.

1 2 3 4 5 6 7 8 9 10 R 25 24 23 22 21 20 19 18 17 16

Photographs ©: cover: Hugo Van Lawick/National Geographic Creative; 3 top left: Feng Yu/Shutterstock,
Inc.; 3 top right: Simone-/Thinkstock; 3 bottom: Eric Isselée/Thinkstock; 4: Michael Nichols/National
Geographic Creative; 8, 11: Jane Goodall Institute; 12: Mint Images/Superstock, Inc.; 15: Jane Goodall
Institute; 19: Hugo Van Lawick/National Geographic Creative; 20: Anup Shah/Nature Picture Library;
23: CSU Archives/Everett Collection/Rex USA; 24: John Giustina/Photoshot; 27: David S. Holloway/Getty
Images; 28: NHPA/Superstock, Inc.; 30 left: Jane Goodall Institute; 30 right: Michael Nichols/National
Geographic Creative; 31 top: Guenter Guni/iStockphoto; 31 center top: Flirt/Superstock, Inc.; 31 center
bottom: Michael Nichols/National Geographic Creative; 31 bottom: Jose Luis Pelaez/Media Bakery.

Maps by XNR Productions, Inc.

Table of Contents

Meet Jane Goodall

Jane Goodall has the coolest job on Earth! She gets to work outside. She travels all over the world. And, best of all, her coworkers are chimpanzees!

For more than 50 years, Goodall has studied chimps. She has made amazing discoveries. And she has spent her life trying to protect these amazing animals in the wild.

Jane Goodall was born on April 3, 1934, in London, England. When she was five, her family moved to a town by the sea. Jane loved exploring outside. Even as a child, she loved animals.

FAST FACT!

When Jane was one, her father gave her a toy chimpanzee. She named it Jubilee. Jane took it with her everywhere.

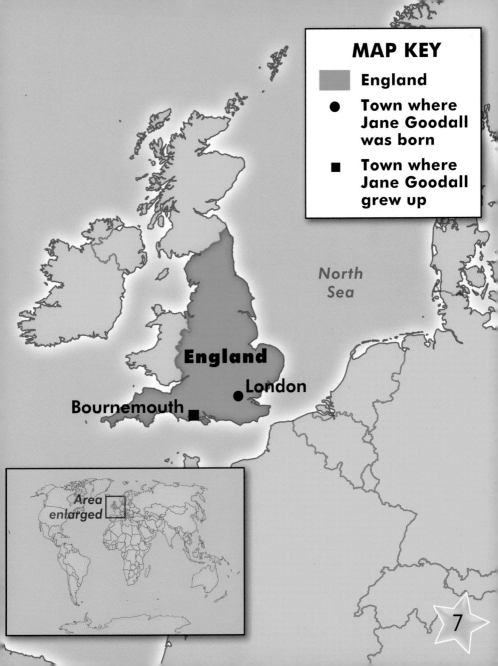

MAP KEY

England

● Town where Jane Goodall was born

■ Town where Jane Goodall grew up

North Sea

England

London

Bournemouth

Area enlarged

Jane's family had a chicken coop in their yard. Once, when she was young, Jane sat in the coop for four hours. She was waiting to see an egg hatch! No one knew where she was. Her parents called the police to help them find her. Jane knew she wanted to work with animals someday.

This photo shows Jane as a little girl. That is Jubilee next to her.

Jane also knew she wanted to travel to Africa. She had read about it in her favorite stories. At that time, it was very rare for a woman to travel to faraway places. It was very rare for a woman to have a job that took her on big adventures.

After high school, Jane became a secretary. It was a way to earn money. But it was not Jane's dream.

Jane poses with Rusty, a neighbor's dog. The dog was her good friend!.

A Dream Come True

Then, when she was 23, something amazing happened to Goodall. Her high school friend had moved to Africa. She lived in a country called Kenya. The friend invited Goodall to visit. One of her dreams was coming true!

Some of the most incredible animals on the planet live in Kenya.

Soon Goodall met the famous scientist Dr. Louis Leakey. He was getting ready to start a study of chimpanzees. He gave Goodall a job as his secretary.

Before long, Leakey noticed her interest in animals. He changed her job. Now Goodall's job would be to study chimpanzees. But first Leakey needed to raise money to pay for his study.

Here is Jane Goodall
with Dr. Leakey.

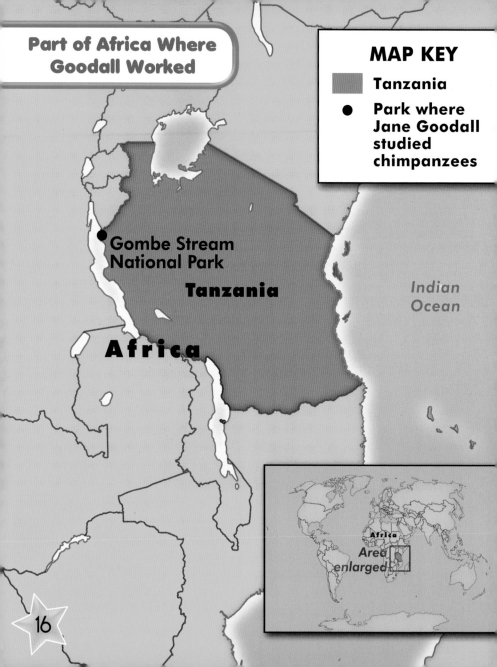

Part of Africa Where Goodall Worked

MAP KEY

Tanzania

● Park where Jane Goodall studied chimpanzees

● Gombe Stream National Park

Tanzania

Indian Ocean

Africa

Africa

Area enlarged

16

In the meantime, Goodall went back to England. She got a job at the London Zoo. Whenever she had time, she **observed** the zoo's chimpanzees. She watched them closely.

Two years later, Goodall returned to Africa. Dr. Leakey got the money he needed. It was time for Goodall to start studying the chimpanzees. Her life's work was beginning!

Living with Chimps

At first, the chimps did not let Goodall get close. She had to observe them from a far-off hill. It was a frustrating way to work.

She started to use bananas to win over one chimp. He was a male she had named David Greybeard. The other chimpanzees saw that David trusted Goodall. They began to trust her, too.

Goodall with David Greybeard

FAST FACT!

Goodall learned that chimps have families and friends, just as humans do. They feel happiness and sadness. They play games. They go to war. They hug and kiss.

Goodall spent all of her time with the chimpanzees. She discovered many things that no one had known before. She saw chimps using sticks to dig for termites. Before her discovery, people thought only humans used tools.

Goodall also saw chimpanzees eating meat as well as plants. Scientists had always thought they were **vegetarians**.

These discoveries made Goodall famous.

Goodall's life was busy. She married a wildlife photographer, and they had a son. She also got a college degree and wrote a book. When her first marriage ended, Goodall married again. The whole time, she kept studying chimps.

Here is Goodall with her son. His nickname was "Grub."

Making a Difference

Goodall worked with chimpanzees for many years. She began to see that she needed to do more than study them.

Chimpanzees are an **endangered species**. Goodall wanted to protect them. She knew she needed to protect their **habitat**. In 1977, she created the Jane Goodall Institute. Its goal is to study and protect chimpanzees and their homes.

In 1991, Goodall created a group just for children. It is called Roots & Shoots. Roots & Shoots teaches children to care for their environment, their communities, and animals. All around the world, its members are making a difference.

Goodall talks to kids about how they can help make a difference.

Timeline of Jane Goodall's Life

1957
goes to Africa; meets Dr. Louis Leakey

1934
born on April 3

1960
begins studying chimpanzees

Jane Goodall is in her 80s. She is still working hard for chimpanzees and for our planet.

She says, "Every individual matters. Every individual has a role to play. Every individual makes a difference. And we have a choice: What sort of difference do we want to make?"

1967
gives birth to son

1991
starts Roots & Shoots

1987
starts the Jane Goodall Institute

A Poem About Jane Goodall

She watches chimpanzees
as quietly as you please,
and asks you to give a hand
to help protect their land.

You Can Help Protect Animals

- Think of ways you can help animals. You can be kind to the animals you meet. You can volunteer at an animal shelter.

- Get your friends and neighbors interested in helping, too.

Glossary

endangered species
(en-DAYN-jurd SPEE-sheez):
animal or plant whose numbers
are so small it is in danger of
dying out completely

habitat (HAB-uh-tat): where an
animal lives and makes its home

observed (uhb-ZURVD): watched
closely and paid careful attention

vegetarians (vej-uh-TER-ee-uhns):
people or animals who do not
eat meat or animal products

Index

Facts for Now

Visit this Scholastic Web site for more information on Jane Goodall:
www.factsfornow.scholastic.com
Enter the keywords **Jane Goodall**

About the Author

Jodie Shepherd, who also writes under the name Leslie Kimmelman, is an award-winning author of dozens of books for children, both fiction and nonfiction. She is a children's book editor, too.